The Power
of the
Present Moment

Peter Sammarco

Published By

Trafford
PUBLISHING

To order products and services directly please contact
www.healyourself.ca / www.fivepillars.ca or email peter@fivepillars.ca

Some products or services are available at special quantity discounts for bulk
purchases for sales promotions, premiums, fund raising, or educational use.
Special books or book excerpts also can be created to fit special needs.

All writings are Peter Sammarco's opinions and thoughts.

❀ ❀ ❀

Order this book online at www.trafford.com/07-0786
or email orders@trafford.com

Most Trafford titles are also available at major online book retailers.

Note for Librarians: A cataloguing record for this book is available from Library
and Archives Canada at www.collectionscanada.ca/amicus/index-e.html

Printed in Victoria, BC, Canada.

ISBN: 978-1-4251-2437-3

*We at Trafford believe that it is the responsibility of us all, as both individuals
and corporations, to make choices that are environmentally and socially sound.
You, in turn, are supporting this responsible conduct each time you purchase a
Trafford book, or make use of our publishing services. To find out how you are
helping, please visit www.trafford.com/responsiblepublishing.html*

*Our mission is to efficiently provide the world's finest, most comprehensive
book publishing service, enabling every author to experience success.
To find out how to publish your book, your way, and have it available
worldwide, visit us online at www.trafford.com/10510*

www.trafford.com

North America & international
toll-free: 1 888 232 4444 (USA & Canada)
phone: 250 383 6864 ✦ fax: 250 383 6804
email: info@trafford.com

The United Kingdom & Europe
phone: +44 (0)1865 722 113 ✦ local rate: 0845 230 9601
facsimile: +44 (0)1865 722 868 ✦ email: info.uk@trafford.com

10 9 8 7

This Book is lovingly dedicated to all parents of this world and especially to Peter Sammarco's Mother and Father: Pasquale and Serafina Sammarco.

FORWARD………………

"WHAT WE FEEL WE ATTRACT;

AND WHAT WE VISUALIZE

AND WHAT WE IMAGINE WE BECOME"

~ PETER SAMMARCO

Table of Contents:

The Power of the Present Moment

Part I ~ Quotes

The beauty of nature. We can hear the sounds of the ocean and the birds and listen to the trees as they flutter in the wind and just knowing that we're all connected with one another and that what happens on this side of the ocean just impacts even the other side.

It is like the ripple of water effect. When a drop of water falls down, it creates that ripple effect. So is your love and your kindness. Whether you're running a corporation or whether you're in the community helping children or young adults or the seniors. Whatever it is, know that we're all one. We're all connected and we all love one another and care for one another. As we do that, we show that we care for our planet and we care for ourselves. We're able to create more prosperity, more infinite wealth and more abundance in our world and be able to share with others.

As we're able to provide it for ourselves and the service of others, we find that as we keep giving, we have more to give. And as we acquire, what's important in acquiring is to be able to share it. It's in that service that matters. It's not in the acquiring of the abundance. It's how do we take that and serve it to our family, to our friends, to our associates, and to humanity in general. Have a great day and enjoy the spirit that works through you and within each of us. Ciao for now. Bye-bye.

❋ ❋ ❋

Forgiveness comes when we allow others to be more of who they are without condemnation. Have a great day.

❋ ❋ ❋

Friends increase your self-worth. They do not compete with you. They guide you. They care for you. They listen to you and they love you for who you are and who you're becoming. Friends don't bring you down or criticize you. Don't do it to yourself either. So

---

remember, friends trust your judgment and generally want to see only your deepest desires come true. Why? For they care and bring out the best in you as well as revealing anything that needs to be learned. Friends always stand by your side. Be your own best friend and stand by your own side and listen to the answers that come to you. Make decisions that reveal your truest, highest nature. Bye-bye.

* * *

We tend to spend so much time in our minds that we forget it's important to transcend our mind and to feel with our hearts. When we are spending that time in academic thinking, that linear mind, yes, it's important, but it's also important to remember we need to transcend the mind, transcend linear thinking, and come from a place from the heart, the spirit, a place that allows us to speak from our heart and not just from our academic upbringing. As we do this we're also allowed to allow more of our feelings to show and to share, to be able to come from a place of infinite life and infinite riches.

The infinite wealth that we have in our life is not just based on monetary success, but it's based on our ability to just love who we are and where we are in our life and to enjoy the process. When we enjoy the process and take the time to smell those flowers and smell those roses and pass it on to a friend or to your wife or husband or to a girlfriend or boyfriend, whatever it may be, we're coming from a place of kindness. And in that kindness comes our ability to grow. And in growth, it usually comes for our ability to see change and to grow from it and to transcend difficult moments. As we love, we grow. And as we let go of the past and transcend it, we also grow. It's so very important to be in the moment, to love in the moment, and to care in the moment. When we're too much into the future, we're nearly always too concerned with what's going to happen next, with what the outcome might be, and that causes us worry. When we're too much into the past, we start worrying about little things that are not important, and it becomes almost a concern of fear. And our past also doesn't allow us to transcend and be in the moment, and it also brings us down. It makes us sad. It makes us feel we're not worthy at times because we're constantly mumbling and jumbling through the past and thinking, "Oh, I could have done it this way. I should have done it that way. Darn this." And it doesn't work.

The reality is we mustn't spend too much time in the past and we must not spend any time in the future. And as we spend more time in the moment, we're able to understand that happiness comes from living in this moment.

* * *

My intention, thought, and prayer is that this book will help you to see things another way and develop sensibility to grow and to change your life in love, caring, compassion for yourself and others.

Living in the moment, loving in every moment, forgiving one's self will allow others to forgive us. Embrace your mistakes, your errors, or your knowledge and allow it to flow through you and then out of you. You can only, only, only hold on to good once you have embraced your dangers, angers, and fearful thoughts, hatred, and allowed it to flow through. Embrace it. And it will love -- allow yourself to feel what you feel. Embrace it and then now you can embrace the new and the old has left your body and left your consciousness forever and forever. Ciao for now.

* * *

Hello. As I listen to the birds and the trees and I listen to the voice of God that works within us, hear the words and the ocean and love one another in peace and in tranquility. Listen closely as you hear the voice of God and the birds and the trees and know we are one with it all.

* * *

Hello. Be in the moment and understand that when we spend too much time in the past, we find ourselves very bad and melancholy to the point of clinical depression. So it's so important for us to not be concerned about the past because our past is over.

What's important is that we present as much of our energy in this moment. If we spend too much time in the future, what happens also is that we become worried and anxious. The clinical word, of course, is anxious.

Another thing is we get worried rather than being in the moment. So if we spend too much time in Western culture, which thinks about the future, and Eastern culture, which thinks about the present, we need to realize that it's important to also kind of have a balance of the two and not be so caught up in the past, but understand that you learn from your past and it allows you to see your future. Have a great day and we'll speak to you soon. Bye-bye for now.

※ ※ ※

Cultivating, love and kindness in our relationships.

※ ※ ※

It's funny -- it's late at night now. 2:30 or so. And I was at the Thrifty's in Tsawassen after I dropped off Rose and it was amazing the genius of Kaitlin, a person working where I got the food for Kinoe. I was in aisle five and I could hear she liked to read. So I told her I wrote a book and it's coming out on May 5. And she went to me "That's my birthday. That's when my birthday is." Just another coincidence that keeps happening every day. And I'm just very blessed. I have to remember that. Okay. Bye.

※ ※ ※

These were done last weekend on a hot, warm, sunny day. Today is now May 30, Memorial Day, Monday, in the United States of America, 2005. [currently I am in Vancouver, British Columbia, Canada] What I wanted to talk about in this current new book is the importance of understanding how while walking through the aisles of magazine shops and grocery stores, I've noticed how many magazines are tailored to women to teach them not how to love. To come from fear. How men really are. What men do. Creating the separation between men and women to the extent of creating already a separation between them in relationships.

These magazines and these shows on television that are on frequently that are not on Public Television have a tendency -- and I won't mention any names of types of shows -- they have a tendency to bring people down, to be argumentative. They do not show forms of love, care, and compassion. They seem to show the individuals as being great people and then being destroyed by an individual based on evildoers and that they can't take care of themselves and that something will always happen -- something bad will happen. Even when things are good, something bad will happen.

And magazines do the same. They say all the little secrets that you should know about married men. Things of this nature. Or what you need to know about making your man fulfilled. No. What you need to do is come from a place of what fulfills you and how do you care for the people around you.

Are you and your partner best friends? Do you share the same values, value system? Do you love each other for who you are? Do you love the essence of each other's nature? Are you willing to appreciate each other's differences? Will you tolerate through those challenges and differences that you may have between your husband and your wife or between a partner or a couple? Are you willing to forgive when things are difficult?

Are you willing to understand that sometimes people may have done or said things that they didn't mean, but that doesn't make them a terrible person for the rest of their lives, but maybe that behavior was not appropriate? And will you tolerate that once in a while and forgive them or are you going to continually bring it up, bring up the past in order to control them or in order to be right rather than choosing to be kind, loving, and come from a place of peace?

What are the choices you're going to make? Those are the kinds of magazines and books as well as T.V. shows that need to be shown to the public, to women, to men, to children, to share loving kindness, to show that -- where do you want to come from? Do you want to come from fear or do you want to come from love? Do you want to come from doubt or do you want to come from knowing and Certainty? Do you want to come from beliefs or do you want to come from knowing? Do you want to have all this constant doubt or do you want to have this constant knowing within you? Do you want to be able to be the destiny of your own future? Do you want to be able to sit down and understand who you are? Do we want to empower people to become more of who they are or less of who they are? These are the kinds of questions we need to ask ourselves. Do we want our partners to become greater and stronger human beings or do we want them to stay the same, like everybody else or someone else so this way they won't change, so this way we can feel comfortable?

Where is that fine line? The key is you allow your partner to be more of who they are. You allow them to grow. And if you're with the right person, you will always grow together and you allow each other to grow at your own pace. When someone grows more than the other, there's a tendency for the relationship to separate. I come that they might have life and that they might have it more abundantly. John 10, Verse 10. Amen. June 2, 2005.

※ ※ ※

Seek out the best in others, not the worst in others. Seek out to bring out what you can in others in an area in their life where their weaknesses become their strengths. Have a great day.

In our body what do you think — which area of the body heals the wound? It is always the weakest part of the body that heals the wounds and the strongest part of the body that maintains the body. So the maintenance of the body is maintained by the strongest points of the body and the weakest part of the body where the cut exists is exactly where the healing begins.

Well, the same goes in many cases when we see someone ill. How come we see that one who is ill maybe consoling someone who is feeling the loss of the person who is ill? This is very common.

※ ※ ※

We all have lessons to learn and we learn from them. We all make mistakes, but there really are no mistakes. They're all divinely set up in order for us to grow. Be thankful for that and learn from the situation that you've created in your life and take a moment to be thankful again that you have learned something that allows you to share with others.
We learn from our lessons in life. Go forward. Do not look back. And always spend as much time as you can in the present and be

happy because in the end, all that matters is what you do in this very moment and how you invest your energy in this moment will transform into where your future will lie in the end. But know in the end there is no end, but it is how we take the time to spend as much peace and joy and happiness in this moment that allows us to move forward and propel to the next level of our living and breathing consciousness and sub-consciousness. It helps us to grow to higher and more spiritual beings than ever before.

* * *

Give in this moment and see how it makes you feel. See how it brings you joy and see how it creates more peace in your inner world and in the world around you. This peace will resonate in this whole global village called life just by your intention of giving from a peaceful and loving heart.

Allow yourself in any relationship to be more of who you are in the relationship, not less of who you are.

* * *

Infinite riches and abundance comes in what we choose to attract into our lives. Do we choose to attract more love and compassion and understanding into our lives and maintain that level of kindness in our lives or do we choose to see what we don't want and what we can't have and what we see and do we wish to attract those kind of negative feelings and emotions?

For reality is that the law of attraction is just based on just that. What you envision to see and what you want to feel in your heart is what you become. So choose things that you want. Feel them in your heart. Visualize they're already here. Live it like as if it's already here. And inevitably it is and you create your own world and your own reality. So be the creator of your own world today and choose to feel what you want and what you feel you need and it will be attracted to you in the desires and avalanches of amounts all in divine order based on your own creation. Thank you. Namaste.

* * *

I feel and I know that we can just heal ourselves by doing nothing. All we need to do is feel it inside. I feel that we can just do nothing and we will feel the healing inside. When the intention is done with love, we can heal every part of our body, every molecule and every distinct atom can be transformed in an instant based on how we feel and how we transcend our mind and go back to our spirit that heals our inner being at all times. [June 3, around 4:00-ish a.m.]

(The quote I said to a friend, "I kind of feel we can just say nothing and you will feel the healing inside." Lots of love to you....)

Anyhow, the point being that we need to understand that we can heal ourselves. And usually the best way of healing is through silence. In that silence we're able to create those molecules that seem like reality and transform those thoughts or feelings into matter and create healing within our own bodies. And this is what's so important and fundamental to learn, that we can heal our body ourselves without the practice of any other forms. It can be done with the balance between the practitioner and our ability to heal ourselves.

A good example of that is Qigong, of course.

❊ ❊ ❊

We can generate loving kindness in every relationship that we have and in our ability to relinquish our ego comes in our ability to generate loving kindness and cultivate loving kindness in all the relationships around us. Have a great day and do so today. Generate that love and cultivate it to all others around you today. *

❊ ❊ ❊

Our ego always wants us to be right, to try to prove someone else wrong as Wayne Dyer says. Now, this truth, do we choose to be kind or do we choose to be right. This is all a choice.

❊ ❊ ❊

See yourselves as already the way you want to be. Again, see yourself already as the way you want to be. What you see in me you see in you. You have what you see in me. What you want to be opened in me is what you want to see opened in you. So remember, what you see in others is what you see in yourself.

❊ ❊ ❊

Find your love in yourself. It is the only place you will find it.

* * *

It's not the only place you'll find it. Find your love in yourself. You'll find it everywhere around you and within you first.

* * *

Here we go. Find your love in yourself and everywhere around you.

(June 8, 2005, 10:51 p.m.)

THE END

Part II ~ Quotes

When you give, you give from the heart of love and light.

❊ ❊ ❊

Love, when you find it in your heart, you will find it in your mind. It is then you can transcend the mind and live in the moment with love always in mind where there will be positive change once we transcend the mind and feel from our hearts. Our hearts heal our world and our wounds.

❊ ❊ ❊

When we give from our heart, nothing else matters. When we pray for our friends and when we pray for our enemies and we decide to make changes from our minds to ones where we love, it is in this time we find miraculous changes in our world.

❊ ❊ ❊

When we are angry, it is this that stands in the way of love. When we relinquish our need to be concerned about our past or being right, then we move forward and relinquish all of our illusions and live from a relationship that is based on love and quiet our hearts and minds, allowing us to live in constant blissfulness and inner peace.

❊ ❊ ❊

Sometimes it is in our hearts that we feel that we may not understand, but always remember that time is actually nonlinear because a lot of what's going on is all taken care of in divine order. So understand that the heart usually penetrates in a way that allows us to see things that we didn't want to see in our minds.

❊ ❊ ❊

Our hearts heal us of our wounds, heal us of our pain, and heal us of our concerns of the periphery as we realize the center of our soul and our spirit starts and remains with our own hearts.

❊ ❊ ❊

Life begins and starts with us as we know. And as we continue to slice the layers of negativity and throw them into the ocean or into the water, in whatever analogy we may use, know that you can do anything. So as you follow your heart and your spirit always knows where you need to go.

* * *

Follow your dreams. Follow your visions and know that in the end, no matter what anyone says, you know what's best. No one knows what's best. So follow your endeavors, follow your spirit, follow your guides, and follow your vision and see in the end that all that really matters is what you feel in your heart and what you desire that you are destined to do. You only know what is best for you.

* * *

Remember that we are God within us all. Know that you can do all things from within. Resonating within you in abundance and avalanches of understanding and wealth consciousness comes in our ability to listen to our subconscious mind and allow that subconscious mind to lead our conscious mind in the direction of our dreams and endeavors, knowing that at the end, the spirit is the subconscious and our hearts are what matters the most. It is our hearts and our spirits that allows our subconscious mind to create the greatest endeavors in mankind's history. Do the same and follow your heart and you will always have the vision that will create miracles.

* * *

We are all here to achieve greatness. We are all here to create greatness. We are all here to dominate our own destiny. No one else's but our own.

* * *

Know that you are God in all that you are, all that you do, and all you can be.

* * *

Create your own destiny by following your own heart's desires.

* * *

Love who you are and know that all that matters is in loving yourself. You can look forward to being together in the same direction of those who love you.

* * *

Follow your dreams. Follow your vision and know in the end your heart will always tell you what is right for you.

* * *

Infinite riches and infinite wealth is something that starts from our own infinite abundance and our willingness to love ourselves.

* * *

What we give to others is usually a very good indication of what we give to ourselves. What we give to ourselves is usually a good indication of what we give to others. So give generously and follow your heart and know in the end that what matters is the abundance of wealth that we give to one another. Wealth is an inside job.

* * *

When we follow our heart and know that we are doing what we love, then we can say truly we do not need to work another day in our lives. Do what you love and the desire to do what you love will always allow you to acquire the monetary success you've only dreamed of.

* * *

Know that you are so powerful and capable of doing anything on this planet. Know you can do anything with the desire that allows you to follow your dreams and visions from within.

* * *

Our love and our light allow us to create the glue that holds the Universe together, which is always our hearts, never our minds.

* * *

Beyond love there is a seed of universal consciousness, a seed that allows us to see beyond what we've ever seen before. It is in this vision that we need to follow our dreams and know that we can create anything in our world.

* * *

In giving, we see that we have the ability to continually give without any loss whatsoever. So know in giving you always have more to give, and it is in this giving that you know that you truly love not only humanity, but yourself. But most importantly, yourself.

* * *

God within us listens to every prayer. Think of the analogy of the television set. When we turn on the converter or the remote control, what happens? The television goes on. What proof do we have that the television goes on? Do we see the ray that hits from the remote control to the television? No. We can't see it, so how can we prove it. But we know it works. The same goes for prayer. We may not be able to see how prayer works, but we know that once we use it, it is just like soap. The more you use it, the more you cleanse. And the more you wash yourself, the cleaner you are. So is prayer. Prayer works in a fundamental way. The more you use it, the more it works.

* * *

We are all here to continue down our divine purpose. And once we allow this to unfold, we see the divinity that is within each one of us.

* * *

God allows us this great affirmation that as we multiply in God's abundance within us, we allow it to increase exceedingly within us in infinite abundance.

* * *

Realize that God is infinite and it's within each one of us, the spirit and the source that is blessing us in nature and the infinite ability to respond to all of our concerns upon its request.

* * *

God knows how to open our hearts because it is within the divine within each one of us to see the good in each one of us and within us day by day and allowing the past to transcend and allowing us to live in the very moment that is divine and pure in every way.

* * *

As we know, "ask and it shall be given to you..." as Matthew 7:7 says. But know this is the form of prayer and meditation. When you ask in meditation for what you desire, it will always manifest in the greatest abundance that one probably hasn't even imagined....

❊ ❊ ❊

As we allow our ability to create our imagination we allow ourselves the expectancy that comes from the benefit of taking the time to be at peace and follow the inner knowing that guides us all.

❊ ❊ ❊

Inner peace is given to us all, but it is only when we allow the periphery to influence us that inner peace might be destroyed.

❊ ❊ ❊

Listen to your inner voice in quiet and in confidence and you will always know that this is the greatest ability that one can have, to listen with inner peace and with confidence, because it is in confidence that we have confidence in our confidante.

❊ ❊ ❊

The light of the sun warms our cheeks and our face. So does our love and our light that we give to others. The more we give our love to others, the more we allow others to shine and to receive the greatness that we already know lies within each one of us.

❊ ❊ ❊

Think prosperity and come with whole-hearted thoughts of abundance and watch what happens in the wonders of your prayer that you choose today. Watch what happens to you when you pray for wonders of love and light into your life. It is in doing so that we contemplate the love that creates all of us in this universe today.

❊ ❊ ❊

It is in our giving that we know we have even more to give away. So keep on giving and make sure that first you give to yourself the love and abundance that you are. Say an affirmation as follows. You are a genius, fantastic, incredible spirit, and you can do anything.

❊ ❊ ❊

Here is a prayer. Our infinite intelligence that is guiding us all is also the greatest power that we can ask for when in trouble. Know it is this infinite intelligence that will always guide us in the greatest endeavor that we wish to achieve, which always, always starts from within us.

* * *

We know that love casts out fear as it says in I John 4:18: "Perfect love casts out fear." If you're coming from fear, then truly you are not coming from love.

* * *

What is important to you? To be worrisome and fearful and to continue these patterns or do you wish to come from a place of peace and tranquility that governs your soul and your spirit. Which one will it be today?

* * *

It is in following our hearts that we see the true nature of who we really are.

* * *

In giving and in loving we know that we always have more to give and love to give to others.

* * *

Embrace our past, embrace our darkness. Let it go by loving and learning from our past. As we transcend our past, we are able to live in the moment.

* * *

Love yourself today. Love yourself in this moment. What matters the most is what you choose to do in this very moment. How do you intend to spend your day today? Where do you intend to invest your energy? Always invest it in places that bring you inner peace and love and joy and the harmony that you choose will always be one based on wisdom that comes from love.

* * *

The more that we find that we have time to give to ourselves the infinite patience we wish to give to others, the more we see that others will give us the same. And in doing so we find we have more power and more ability to give not only to others, but to ourselves what we need the most, which is love.

* * *

It is in loving ourselves that we know that we are truly rich.

❀ ❀ ❀

We create loving kindness by generating it within ourselves first.

❀ ❀ ❀

How do we generate loving kindness? We first start by loving who we are, forgiving ourselves for what we have done, and knowing that if we do not even condemn ourselves, there will be no need to even judge or condemn ourselves.

❀ ❀ ❀

Be kind to yourself in friendship. This truly creates the miracles that we really are.

❀ ❀ ❀

Be open to your emotions today. Allow the emotions that you need to feel. Don't control them because if you control them, they will control you. So in doing so, by allowing those emotions to come out, you allow them no longer to control you.

❀ ❀ ❀

When we embrace the emotions that we feel that may have hurt others or ourselves, we allow ourselves to be kind to ourselves and learn from the behavior that may have not been our true identity. In doing so, we see the light again that at one time seemed only darkness.

❀ ❀ ❀

Forgiveness comes in loving ourselves. When we can look at the changes and patterns of our past and let them go gently and kindly, we create the miracle that we are within each one of us.

❀ ❀ ❀

Give from the wealth of abundance that we call life. The more we give to others, the more life gives willingly to us peace harmony and tranquility. Love will continue to expand our spirits and our minds, yet love is not a thought. Love is not even a feeling. It is a mighty energy, an invisible power that gives us our life. The more we give love away, the more we have to give away. And I'll repeat this principle over and over again to impress upon you how important it is to give love.

* * *

The outer world is like the periphery of an atom. The negativity of the outer periphery is not necessarily the most important part. But how that atom bounces from one area to another changes the molecules and particles that surround it. So know that even in our thoughts and in our minds and in our hearts we can change everything instantaneously, impacting all the people around us in our presence.

* * *

Our hearts are what creates the greatest healing and the healing that comes within us is like particles in the atmosphere that generate more infinite abundance into our lives as we generate alignment and love with all of the particles that we choose to create in our world. The attraction of one molecule will bounce and create more of the same molecules and atoms that generate the matter to create instantaneously what we choose to desire in our lives.

* * *

It is true that if we choose to feel good within us all, we choose inner peace within us all. In giving this inner peace to ourselves, we allow others the same in their own world.

* * *

When we choose to be happy for others, we choose to be happy for ourselves. When we choose to be unhappy for others, we create an instant blockage that will destroy not only their world, but our own. Instead, choose kindness and love. Choose to create infinite abundance in their world and see the infinite abundance be created in your own world.

* * *

The greatest act of love is one that comes from unconditional love. It is in doing so that we find the spirit that resides within each one of us.

* * *

Serenity comes in our willingness to grow in synergy with one another.

* * *

We need to be able to create "inter-independent" relationships with one another, creating love with one another rather than creating man-made separations and distinctions. When we make judgments on others it shows how little we choose to be compassionate and caring for others. Forgive ourselves for that and allow new ways and modes of thinking to seep into and seed your heart and allow your subconscious mind to work for you rather than against you.

* * *

Once your ego is gone and you let it go, it is only spirit that can guide you now and forever. It is love that is a part of you that lives within you and within us all and allows us to give the love to yourself and all around you, and to all the people around you.

* * *

Unconditional love comes when we first give love to ourselves and in doing so we allow ourselves the ability to give that love to others.

* * *

Follow your dreams and your visions to the highest regard. Your mission in life is a miracle. Once you have done this with intended action, it is a reality. No longer a vision or a dream, for you are pursuing it with vigor and enthusiasm and allowing the spirit to work through you to completion.

* * *

Know your purpose is always to have fun in what you do. Enjoy the process for in many ways we know that we never complete what needs to be done, but we always will enjoy the process if we choose to do what our heart desires and tells us what we are destined to do.

* * *

How do we learn to love? Love is simple. It is not something complicated. It is not even something we need to even study. Love just is. Love is just being loved. For love is an energy willingly given by our thoughts and our hearts about ourselves. Self-love and the love for all others must always come from unconditional love.

* * *

What is unconditional love? It is our ability to love someone even when we feel that person is not deserving of our love. Everyone is deserving of our love and no one ever is excluded. Simply said, love to love and miracles come. Some of us do not believe in miracles. Fine. Then don't. You can choose what to think, believe, and learn in life. Everyone has a choice to forgive and to love and to expand that love and give it away. Anything we give away multiplies and thus we have more to give.

* * *

"Love, peace, and understanding creates more love in our lives." Lama Margaret Ludwig (a dear friend in Victoria, BC Canada)

* * *

Cultivating love starts by loving those you do not like. Love is simple, simple, simple. "To give wisdom is to love oneself. To keep understanding is to prosper." Proverb 19:18.

* * *

We give as we take in the sweet fresh air of the sun, moon, and starlit sky that is looking down upon us. In those stars are our dreams. We need to direct our emotions towards our long range purpose or personal dream. In doing so, we become close to God or, mildly put, we get in touch with our inner world.

* * *

We get in touch upon divine love and light within us. We get to know who we are and we get to share that with God, who dwells within us. If we remember the importance of giving in to our desires, life will be full of more love. Desires are not evil or bad. They are the essence of life that makes us grow and propels and compels us to prepare for the next level of our dreams, visions, and endeavors.

* * *

We can put these into action by owning our true desires. Our dreams are our own actions. An action can include silence, and inaction for even in inaction we are processing our inner guidance for the action we will need to proceed forward in our dreams and endeavors and our hearts and desires that come from the spirit that resides within each one of us.

* * *

For happy is he who loves himself. Oh, yes, we know how true that is. We cannot love others until we love ourselves. We cannot choose to be in a relationship and it is then we will be happy or when we have the perfect position. We need to be happy with where we are today now in this moment and thus it allows us to enhance the happiness when other things come forward into our lives.

* * *

Those things that come forward into our lives in infinite abundance and avalanches of amounts are something we need to be thankful for. The more thankful we are, the more abundance and infinite patience we will have towards creating constant and never-ending love and infinite abundance in our world and in everyone else's world around us.

* * *

As we know, a child usually watches his parents and whatever the parents do, they tend to do the same. Watch yourself today. See what you've done. What are your actions and behaviors? Have you conducted in a way that allows you to become a greater person or a person who maybe needs to improve in some way? Always ask yourself empowering questions in the morning and the evening and be thankful for all that you have in this moment.

* * *

Riches come when we truly love ourselves. It in loving ourselves we create infinite riches in our world and in the world around us. Infinite riches comes when we know that we truly love ourselves.

* * *

Remember that love is a mighty energy, an invisible force that creates healing all around us and within us all.

* * *

The power to give is truly the power to live.

* * *

When we feel in the morning, do we wish to imagine the ocean and the ocean breeze and the warm air from the sunny skies or do we wish to see and envision destruction in our world? Which one do you believe will bring you inner peace?

* * *

Do we want to create a world of abundance and of creative infinite peace? Start with yourself and see yourself as the creator of your own world and know you can do anything in your own life and thus create more for others in their own lives as well. We truly have an impact on other people's intentions.

* * *

What we find in ourselves is what we will find in other people. So in doing so, we need to ask ourselves these fundamental questions. How have I grown today and how does that make me feel to see that I've become a far more empowering person than yesterday? What have I done today that allows me to learn that I know that I'm a better person than yesterday? And another one is have I chosen to conduct myself in a way that helps me to improve the inner peace and presence that will guide not only myself, but will also impact the presence of others around me.

* * *

Are you thankful this morning for who you are or are you upset that you didn't sleep another hour? Maybe take a moment right now and take a deep breath and say wow, I get a chance to take in another deep breath of fresh air. Be thankful for that for in doing so we know that we are truly alive once again.

* * *

The more we know that we are alive, the more we are able to give our adequate love to all others. We know that we are powerful, but sometimes we feel that we're inadequate in our own love. But we mustn't feel this way. We must realize that our greatness that lies within us lies within each one of us and we need to improve our love and self-esteem for us all. Build each other up to become greater human beings and knowing that in this spirit that creates our greatest endeavors allows us to be who we are today. The True spirit of God that lies within us allows us to do anything and everything. We can create any new project, any new loving thought. As we generate this loving thought within us, we can perpetuate more of this loving kindness to all the people around us.

* * *

Meditation and prayer and all these other forms of calming our mind, clearing our mind, and centering our mind are a way of creating peace and tranquility in our world. Once we transcend all of these behaviors from our mind, we're able to see that our heart is calm and always at peace.

❀ ❀ ❀

As we transcend our minds, we are able to see our inner world clearly.

❀ ❀ ❀

Your inner world is always guided by your heart.

❀ ❀ ❀

Once we know that our inner world is guided by our heart or our spirit or the source within us all, we are able to guide and align with that source at all times. And in doing so, we are able to create the intentions that we wish to desire in our world.

❀ ❀ ❀

God is love and only love. Know thyself is a fundamental principle to knowing how to love and to trust yourself.

❀ ❀ ❀

Once you know who you are, you have no possibility of hurting anyone else. Don't give me the excuse that business is business and that's the way it is. Business involves people. If you have no people, you have no business. You care for one another, not hurt your customers, partners, or clients. It is important to cooperate, not compete. Send love and continued success to your competitors. Give love to your clients. That is crucial to success, wealth, love, and a life worth living.

❀ ❀ ❀

We can try to compete with everyone else, but in reality we're not. We are all unique and have something to give that is uniquely different than everybody else. Once we realize that we can do anything and that we are more than adequate beyond our measures, we are deeply filled with the power that allows us to create the inner world and the outer world that we wish to desire in our continued destiny.

❀ ❀ ❀

The outer world is that of the atom that is negative from the outside periphery. In the center within each of us is a positive force. The positive force is our hearts, and we must listen to that voice in silence and not to the voice behind or in front of us. Instead let us have the power to listen and breathe and go within to know the wisest answers to all of our divinely guided answers awaiting within us. What we all call in the business world our hunches or our intuition. So remember, we need to listen closely to our intuition and hear it once again.

* * *

When we go beyond what the inner world of our universe says, it's best for us to do, we master thyself, our mind is logical and reasonable and intellectual, but trusting in yourself does not come from your brain. It comes truly from your heart.

* * *

When love prevails, nothing else matters. Love makes all things possible. For in God's love and in God there is peace, forgiveness, equanimity, divine, unconditional love.

* * *

Self-confidence is just that. It is faith. When anyone takes our self-confidence, self-love, self-worth, self-esteem, they are in the need of help themselves. Only with love can you let them find themselves. Trust that you are able to help your friends. True friends focus on what a wonderful person you really are.

* * *

Remember that your true friends will always increase your self-worth. They do not compete with you. They guide you, care for you, listen to you, and love you for who you are and who you're becoming. Friends do not bring you down or criticize you. Don't do this to yourself either. They trust your judgments and genuinely want to see only your deepest desires come true. Why? For they care and bring out the best in you as well as reveal anything that needs to be learned. Friends always stand by your side. Be your own best friend and stand by your own side and listen to the answers that come to you. Make decisions based on choices within your own inner guidance. Ask for the inner guidance to help you find the answers that will help guide you to the light and to your journey's destination. Enjoy it along the way.

* * *

Friends see only what's possible. They look at all obstacles yet see only the opportunities. They see only what they know you can do, your own inner strength, God's strength. Together you have synergy.

* * *

Avoiding [frequently using] negative words such as hate is so important. Hate is not of God. The opposite of Love is not more than hate, but fear stemming from that hate. So avoid using that word altogether. When we replace hate, jealousy, envy, or resentment from our minds and use words that fill our hearts with forgiveness, unconditional love, we will see that all things are possible with love in our hearts and God to follow within our hearts. Trust your heart will guide you to where you need to go all in divine order.

* * *

When you know who you are, when you trust in yourself, you know that you have the ability to love yourself. So remember that in following your heart let yourself know that you can do anything & everything. Take a deep breath and be grateful and have great thoughts and great contemplations and visualizations of where you want to be in your own life.

* * *

Trust yourself to know you are divinely guided and know with this power you can do anything & everything you want to achieve in your life. It is wonderful to wake up with a purpose every morning. Know in this infinite prayer of affirmation (your meditation) every day that you are infinitely divinely guided. God is me. I choose to align myself and tap into what is the inner strength and peace the God within me provides. It is given to me in abundance, love, health, peace, success, and wealth. I pray and visualize peace, love, caring, and compassion in the world. I feel it in my body and I am now complete.

* * *

Remember you can do anything in your world. Follow your heart, follow your dreams, and follow your spirit. They will always guide you in the direction that you need to go in infinite abundance.

* * *

Always build yourself up. Trust thyself. Never question your own ability. Build your spirit every day and you will know you can do anything in your world.

※ ※ ※

Let us always choose peace, which may mean not responding at all. Just listening and letting go, like water off a duck's back. God is love and only love. Know thyself is a fundamental principle to knowing how to love and trust yourself. Once you know who you are, you have no possibility of hurting anyone else. Remember that. And in doing so, you know you can do anything & everything once you truly love yourself and give from that wealth of abundance in avalanches and infinite amounts and every day and every way you know you can do anything & everything that you wish to create in your inner world and in your outer world. And this will create an impact in the presence of other people because of what you share and give first and utmost to yourself. This will generate love and penetrate in others as well.

※ ※ ※

Continue growing and know who you really are. Even if you choose not to grow, you will continue to grow anyway, so do not stop just with your gender or your job or your position or what you have. Know that you are more than that. Go beyond that. Transcend all those things and know that your inner self is who you really are. The inner child that you've had every day of your life. Know you can do anything & everything when you listen to that inner child within you. Listen to your dreams as so many others have done the same. You can do it as well.

※ ※ ※

Smile more. It's so important the more you smile and laugh, the more you increase your endorphins and you feel good about yourself. The more you give away that laughter and abundance and smiles, the more you find that it also increases the loving kindness in the presence of others as well. So keep giving your love, your laughter, and your kindness and watch how it will penetrate the world in ways we may have thought unimaginable that are now imaginable.

※ ※ ※

We can give away love or we can give away fear. Which one do you think will create inner peace in your world?

* * *

What we generate in ourselves is what we will generate in others. When we are at peace, we will allow others to feel at peace. It is that simple

* * *

Love is love. There is no other meaning. Nothing could ever be closer to the truth. Babies do not grow in knowledge and then say Okay, now I know who to love. We have the freedom to choose how we react to what happens to us in our lives. Someone may be directing their actions or behaviors towards us that are kind or unkind and we have the power and choice of how we respond to such behavior.

* * *

Embrace whatever you are going through. When you face it, your past or your present moment, it will never control you. Control comes from holding onto the present challenges or mistakes, past mistakes we feel we've made. It is a folly to think that your present or past mistakes are truly mistakes. No. They are not mistakes. No. Let them go. Admit your faults and then move on. Guilt and shame are a waste of our time and energy. This is a valuable energy that needs to be directed towards higher levels of consciousness based on love, joy, forgiveness, and willingness to grow. Always choose energies that bring us closer to inner love and peace and an inner peace that brings us joy and inner harmony.

* * *

When we choose the truth of God within us, we will realize that it is never changing.

* * *

Remember, whatever a man sows, so shall we also reap. And so it is important to sow the good within you and to others and truly you will have the same returned to you.

* * *

God dwells within us all. Know that you are God within and follow the infinite guidance that will allow you to make infinite changes at all times.

* * *

Follow the inner spirit that gives us joy. Allow us the ability to dwell within us the inner spirit that gives us joy.

✳ ✳ ✳

When we refuse to choose for ourselves really what we are saying is we refuse to choose the divinity which is within all of us. We need to make choices knowing that those choices are choices that have been made from within us and allowing our divine guidance to tell us what we need to do next.

✳ ✳ ✳

As we perceive ourselves as individuals that can do anything & everything and that we are truly great spirits, when we see ourselves as great individuals, we allow others to shine as well.

✳ ✳ ✳

Know that who you are is greater than anything in this world.

✳ ✳ ✳

As we follow our inner guidance, we know we can do anything that we choose to put our hearts and minds into doing. Follow that and you will never go wrong.

✳ ✳ ✳

Divine inner healing comes in our choices we make within us. Do we choose to heal and create abundance in our world and abundance in the world around us or do we choose to create a world that takes us away from that? Always choose a world that brings infinite riches to all and infinite wealth also to yourself.

✳ ✳ ✳

As we care we know and think prosperity is possible not only for a selected few, but it is something that is possible within each one of us. Once we choose to generate and stimulate our hearts and minds with thoughts and prayers that are based on thoughts of abundance and beliefs that we can create a healthy life for ourselves based on our own healthy thinking.

✳ ✳ ✳

As we spend less time thinking and heal our world, we know that our hearts do not think. It allows us to do and propel us to do what we need to do next. In action and in peace we will find the action to do what needs to be done next. Follow your heart and enjoy the process and all that we do and all that we are and all that we can be and know that you can do anything everything which is within you and which is within each one of us, the God inner power of peace, power, and love and infinite abundance.

* * *

During a recent discussion we discussed how it is important to love who we are. But how do we do this? Ask ourselves this question. How do you choose to love yourself? Well, simple. Choose not how. Choose not why. Just choose yes. Yes, I will love myself today for I know I am the greatest being in this world and in this planet. I can do anything because I choose the inner world that guides me in all of my endeavors and dreams today.

* * *

Your infinite ability within will always guide you to do better today than you did yesterday. Allow yourself the time to yourself to meditate on this and to contemplate in peace and quiet time to know what needs to be done today and follow that thoroughly to the T.

* * *

Know that abundance and money is circulating in your world at all times. Once you choose to allow it to come into your world wisely and constructively, you allow it in every one else's world. And the more we generate it for others, the more we continue to generate it for ourselves.

* * *

Be thankful for being the creator of your own world. You can create anything in your world once you choose inner peace. And in doing so, you find the inner world will guide you in ways you thought possibly were unimaginable that are now quite capable of giving you the power and the creative source to love money and to know that money is not the root of evil, but to know that in loving ourselves and forgetting to follow the guidance within ourselves is the greatest evil. It is in doing what we love that money will follow and never the other way around.

* * *

Your thoughts create your emotions and inner feelings. Be careful what you think and feel every day for it will become your reality. Choose words that create reality that you wish to feel and love and see every day.

* * *

Success comes to choosing God within you once again as you will serve first. This infinite source will guide you wherever you need to go and to whatever you need in this world. Follow it and you will know you will always be guided in the direction of your dreams and endeavors in infinite abundance of amounts.

* * *

Here is an inner prayer that will guide you. Always know that all wisdom reveals to you the answers that will guide you and show you the way. Be thankful and the right answer will always come and you will always know that the answer is one that will bring you inner peace.

* * *

Follow everything with action, but in doing so first ask yourself and touch your heart, bring your spirit back to yourself and guide me to the miracles which are my birthright every day and I forgive and give in every way that I wish to do so. In my feelings comes my thoughts and creates my prayers every day.

* * *

Know that your feelings and emotions will follow through with thought. So in doing so, remind yourself to choose thoughts that will bring you closer to serving the inner God that's within each one of us.

* * *

Your confidence and riches will fulfill your life in ways that you thought were unimaginable. You can eliminate yourself of sickness and failure and all of the fears and frustrations that are concerning us sometimes on a daily basis that we may call stress. But remember, stress is an illusion we've created in our minds. It was a word that did not even exist 20 years ago. So know that truly it's a word that needs to be eliminated from our vocabulary today. Follow the infinite confidence of riches within us. Know that your confidante is within us and it will give you the confidence to do what you need to do best.

Follow through with that guidance, that infinite riches that's within each of us.

❋ ❋ ❋

I know I am the creator of my own world. Do you know you're the creator of your own world? Choose to be the creator of your own world because your spirit will always guide you in ways that you know will bring you inner peace and generate more peace for the people around you.

❋ ❋ ❋

The day before a business meeting if you have to meet with a colleague or a CEO, pray to that family. Wish them well. Send them love and in knowing the next day once you meet with the CEO of that company or the manager or assistant or other associates that you've created already a miracle the day before in your daily prayer.

❋ ❋ ❋

As we give love to ourselves, we give love to our world.

❋ ❋ ❋

Again, by asking ourselves whether we are willing to break the chains of our past we allow the new to take control completely. We must make this a powerful intention.

❋ ❋ ❋

Do you realize that love comes from your heart? Are you open or closed to loving others and yourself? Where do you put your energy or attention? Which matters most to you? How do you see your priorities in your life? Is your primary purpose to be rich or do you realize you are already rich with love, a sense of humor, intelligence, brilliance, and uniqueness that will astonish the world around you?

❋ ❋ ❋

If I live my purpose and serve others, everything else will take care of itself in divine order.

❋ ❋ ❋

Heal your past and you have mastered yourself through love and forgiveness. Our compassion to ourselves and to others heals our inner world. That is true success. That is mastering thyself.

❋ ❋ ❋

We will always understand that we must learn not to react to other people's opinions, judgments or attacks. That is what true democracy is about, allowing others their own opinions.

＊ ＊ ＊

Although others have their own opinions, understand that it must not waver our own inner peace. Our own inner peace comes from the core within each one of us. That is what brings us inner peace.

＊ ＊ ＊

Have faith in yourself. Faith infinitely moves mountains, which means you trust yourself. When you have faith, trust in something you still have not seen, you are trusting yourself to visualize what you want to see. You see, visualize, and believe in yourself. This trust is deep rooted from within. When you know and trust the infinite divine within, you can create peace all around you. Trust your infinite God within you to create miracles in you and your world.

＊ ＊ ＊

Your true friends care about you and wish the best for you. Be your own best friend and choose the best for yourself and care for yourself in ways that friends care about you.

＊ ＊ ＊

Follow your heart's desire and know that it will bring you inner peace.

＊ ＊ ＊

Love to have your own presence. And in loving your own presence, you will love the presence of others and others will love the presence of you in their lives.

＊ ＊ ＊

There are no accidental meetings. Everyone came in your world for a reason.

＊ ＊ ＊

True prosperity in relationships comes between nations and people once we choose peace and harmony within each one of us.

＊ ＊ ＊

Striving for power or political domination is not what truly leads leaders and countries to the best of their abilities. It is something that is greater than that. It is our ability to strive for the best for others, to wish only the good of others, and to strive to allow people to be more of who they are, not less of who they are. To allow them their own self-reliance. To allow them their freedom to be who they truly want to be. Be your own best friend. Dominate your own world and know that truly dominance of power of this world is not what we need, but it's the inner world of power within us all that we need to exude and use more often and share that with us all, that it is within us all to create more miracles of peace, love, and care for our world and our inner world. Our deepest desire is peace in our inner world.

❋ ❋ ❋

Dreams are made of love and love is made of breath and breath is made of thoughts and thoughts will create our prayers.

❋ ❋ ❋

You will and I will have a creative and productive week. Together we are one.

❋ ❋ ❋

What we see in our world is what we see in the outer world.

❋ ❋ ❋

What we see in our world is what we see in our inner world.

❋ ❋ ❋

Create abundance in your world by being loving and caring and also forgiving of yourself of anything that you've done to yourself and to others.

❋ ❋ ❋

Joy and peace are a choice, and the choice must always come from within.

❋ ❋ ❋

Please maintain your humbleness. It is our key to successful living. Get your creative juices flowing now and every day and acknowledge the inner power that you have within.

❋ ❋ ❋

Be thankful and understand that when you are able to know your own enlightenment and divinity within you, you are more able to spread peace within you and to all. Acknowledge your own divinity and continue to be thankful in the process that you enjoy doing the most. And in doing so, know that you will never have anything complete, but you will always be enjoying the process that brings you closer to inner peace, inner guidance, and strength, that allows others to do the same in their own world. Be an example to others by following your own heart and your own foot steps of your dreams and seed a few other seeds along the way, knowing that you've created a world that is not only great, but greater than you could even have ever imagined once the seeds sprout and germinate into something much greater than all mankind.

＊ ＊ ＊

When we give love and affection to our friends and to our loved ones or to our brothers and sisters, what we are saying is that we wish the same care and love for ourselves. In doing so, we share that love that's within each one of us and we allow ourselves to live in the moment with the utmost love and peace and joy that we all need in our world.

＊ ＊ ＊

Calmness comes from within us all. Calmness comes when we find God within us as well as in the flowers we plant and the roses we give, in the tulips we pluck and the cherry blossoms we admire. Smell flowers, talk with nature, and listen to ourselves.

＊ ＊ ＊

Take time today to hug your friend and remember it's scientifically proven if you have 7 to 12 hugs a day that you increase your hemoglobin levels. So go ahead and hug your friend today. Hug a neighbor. Hug someone you know that truly you can trust and give that love and increase each other's hemoglobin and make each other both feel good about each other's presence in each other's world.

＊ ＊ ＊

Remember that laughter allows us to heal our body and that food is a medicine. So give the food of laughter and abundance to everyone else's world and especially give it to ourselves.

＊ ＊ ＊

When an adult starts crying, do we give them a tissue or do we choose to give them a hug? Always remember the same goes for a child. When a child starts to cry, do we give them a tissue or do we embrace them? Embrace ourselves when we are in tears because it is in this process that we are truly healing.

* * *

When we hug another, we show that we care. When we touch another, we show our love. And in doing so, we heal ourselves and the people around us.

* * *

Trust in yourself and believe and know you will receive the answers. When you believe, answers appear in ways you cannot imagine. In dreams and visions and words or thoughts and answers that are given through others. The voice which means something to you and will guide you to where you need to go.

* * *

Simply take time to listen. Go within and take time to listen. Breathe. Breathe and breathe and breathe, and the answer is always in the air. We need to be willing to make gradual changes every day. Where do we put our attention? We become what we put our attention on. What thoughts do we think about ourselves and others? What kind of questions do we ask ourselves during the day, morning, afternoon, and night? Where have we invested our energy today? Are we thinking and feeling with love and faith or are we investing our energy on negativity, anger, anxiety, or tears. Where is this anxiety coming from? Isn't anxiety just something we've spent too much time doing because we're thinking too much about the future? And sometimes we spend too much time thinking about the past, which makes us melancholy. So remember, follow the present moment. Follow the heart and know in the present moment you will always be at peace and you will always feel happy and you will always be at a place of infinite abundance and bliss in your world and this will generate more love around you in your outer world as well.

* * *

We're learning about showing how love is important in the way we give and what we give is usually that unconditional love to everything and everyone in our thoughts and minds and our hearts always. What kind of questions do we ask ourselves at night and for what purpose do we ask these questions? For we are all here for each other always. Remember that I am also here for you and the spirit within us is connecting us at this moment. Knowing that we can have the power to move mountains and clouds, our subconscious minds affect the environment. Our consciousness truly does affect the environment. Remember this. Give this world and the people in this world your love. Give it away and give it to everyone as we have the consciousness to choose peace and love and prosperity for all of us. And if more of us believe in that, we will all have created this in our world.

* * *

Take the time to read a book on yoga or the scientific study of the power of breath or anything that will bring you some sort of sense of inner joy and peace. Studying God's presence dwelling within us will also help us to search and improve our own vitality and health and personal strength. Do so and you will know that yoga and meditation and prayer work within us all.

* * *

Master yourself through the power of breathing, meditating, yoga, and deep prayer. For in silence so shall I be there residing in you. For you and I are one. Silence always brings us closer to ourselves. It is in breathing and connecting to our hearts that we create peace in our inner world.

* * *

Realign your thoughts to your heart and feel your mind slowly being governed by the stillness and silence of your heart. Our minds produce tens of thousands of thoughts in a day. Many are repeated. We need to reflect our thoughts and discover what we think of ourselves. It's important that we always think good things of ourselves and seed that in others as well.

* * *

Our hearts take us away from our thoughts and our thoughts take you away from your heart. So remember, this world has nothing more to offer you than that which is within us all. Follow your heart and the desires of the heart will heal you.

＊ ＊ ＊

Remember the importance of breath and prayer and then meditate on any question you have for you will find God once you find yourself within silence. The Father will guide you and listen to your voice. As you pray deeply and concentrate on your breath, you will be guided to the answers that await in your time of silence. In silence and prayer so shall I be there. Close your eyes, Be still, and Listen.

＊ ＊ ＊

Know that you are the feeling creator of your own pain in your body and that if you have anger or a headache, you need to ask yourself who does this belong to? Allow yourself to heal your own body and know you can be your own best friend. Physician, heal thyself.

＊ ＊ ＊

We need to ask ourselves more powerful questions. Sometimes people say how can it get better than this. Yes, that's true. How can it get better than this? As you allow yourself to penetrate such a thought, remember, how can it get better than this, and it will always get better than this.

＊ ＊ ＊

Ask yourself every day and in every hour of the day how can I become a better loving, caring spirit human being for my company, for my family, for my friends. In doing so we allow ourselves a constant improvement that allows us to be better individuals on a day-to-day basis.

＊ ＊ ＊

Remember what you have learned today may change tomorrow. So allow yourself that flexibility. When someone asks you what did you know about this or that, always know that you can say tomorrow I may change my mind. My opinion may change. So always know that what you ask today, that tomorrow I may have grown and learned something new and that opinion may change.

＊ ＊ ＊

How can it get better than this? Yes, we're going back to the same question. Ask yourself how it can get better than this and it will. Just watch how it will get better than this. See what happens when you just deliver these powerful words to your heart.

❋ ❋ ❋

Being thankful every morning, God's abundance and avalanches will continue to flow through you and within each one of us every moment of the day when we allow it to do so.

❋ ❋ ❋

Know that God within us will take care of all things. Everything all in divine order, which will always guide us in the divinity of our dreams and endeavors. With love to you and to all know you can make a difference in your world and in the people around you and the friends around you just by choosing to love all, and you will be loved as well at all times.

❋ ❋ ❋

There is so much love in the world. We just need to look around us and see how there are so many others there that care about us as we care about ourselves.

❋ ❋ ❋

Once we take time to take care of ourselves, others will also wish to take care of us. We need to love who we are and in loving who we are, others will love us. In praising who we are, others will praise us. For once we do not praise ourselves, do not expect anyone to praise you. Everything must first start with ourselves. In doing so, we must go within and listen in silence and be guided in that inner silence. Even for one minute or 30 seconds watch what a difference it makes in our world and how that generates loving kindness around us in our inner world and our world around us.

❋ ❋ ❋

Infinite riches are coming to us all in infinite abundance. Know that and create that in your world and in all the people around us, in their world.

❋ ❋ ❋

Infinite riches are coming to us all in limitless abundance.

❋ ❋ ❋

When we care, others will care about us. Remember that no matter how much we know, what's more important is that we care.

* * *

When we give to others, we must not only promise to give what we wish to give to others, but we must also allow ourselves to give even more of what we promise to give. In doing so, we create miracles in our world and in their world, too.

* * *

When we give, we know that we have the ability to also receive. Remember, our ability to receive comes from our willingness to give.

* * *

How we see our world is how others will see our world.

* * *

It is not how much we do that matters, but it is really how much we wish to accomplish on a day-to-day basis.

* * *

And what we accomplish on a day-to-day basis is based on the little steps that we take, the little steps that create the bigger goal always in mind.

* * *

Stop yourself next time you're reacting in a way that's not productive and not serving you any longer. In doing so, we're able to choose another way. And when we choose another way, we're able to see the light once again.

* * *

How we see others is usually how we see ourselves.

* * *

Give into kindness, compassion, and ethical living. Stay away from the rules that direct you away from your love. Live by principles, not rules, to create your peace in your lives. Love will bring far greater rewards than any other thing. Give what you want and you will always find more to give, for love is equal to God. It is infinite, and love is boundless energy with no time strap around it. It is the universal cosmic energy that flows through us all and gives to us all unconditionally.

* * *

Repetition is so important. To unlearn old ways we need to repeat new patterns and ways of thinking and feeling and doing things. So today put a quote on your refrigerator that will empower you to see yourself as the greatest human being possible and know that your spirit will guide you to exactly what needs to be said.

* * *

Give away love and you will always have more to give away. Yes, that's true. Friends believe in you and as you believe in them, they will always be there for you once you first believe in yourself.

* * *

Know that you can do anything & everything. Know that your inner voice will guide you in the greatest direction possible that will be of the greatest benefit to you all in divine order.

* * *

The lighthouse effect. There is the light of love that awaits within us. There is no other power more appealing than love. Love heals all things completely. Without love, you cannot gain wisdom. Love equals wisdom for love is an energy. Knowledge will not gain you wisdom. Only love can bring you closer to understanding knowledge. Love equates to wisdom.

* * *

You cannot love humanity if you hate others. Embrace your hate. Understand it, then toss the hat of hatred gently down the stairs and say good-bye to it and choose to love again like the child wants inside of you.

* * *

Can you be of God or experience like qualities if you hate other people in your heart? Animosity and anger are different. With anger we are dealing with injustice. We are dealing with hurt feelings. Truly hate, which is a very strong word, should be avoided and eliminated from our vocabulary. Remember, when someone is angry, usually they are truly deeply hurt.

There are different forms of anger. There is anger when you feel that an injustice has been done in the world. And that might be a justifiable anger. But knowing that that anger comes from a deep, deep misunderstanding that we do not wish to see the world the way it is, so it might make us angry. Let's always be proactive and find ways to generate that anger to propel us to go into action and doing something that is always positive and proactive in our world and in the world that will impact others around us in our presence and in our actions.

✳ ✳ ✳

Consider the following as an important part of living and loving and a peaceful life. One, an ethical and compassionate life where we forgive ourselves and others, actions of loving kindness, and, two, be in God's presence by helping others and together love ourselves and others. Three, talk to God through prayer. For example, through some sort of Psalms or the Kabbalah or any other spiritual practice you feel comfortable with. Listen to God by breathing in love and giving thyself love and then exhaling to give love away. The next important step is meditation has a profound impact on our lives. Read and be inspired by literature and listen to your inner voice of what it tells you to do next. And the last one, ask yourself questions out loud and listen to the voice in your head and the calmness and peace in your heart. When you feel peace, then you know you have connected with God. God comes from the heart and never from the mind or the head.

✳ ✳ ✳

What we give to others is important. So give thankfulness. Be thankful. When you haven't seen a friend for a while and they've done something for you, the first thing you can do, as done in the Japanese culture, is to be done the moment it has been given. And in so many other cultures, being thankful and gratitude just creates more of that abundance in your world and in the world all around us.

✳ ✳ ✳

Love is not something you can horde or hold on to like some kind of possession, a mistake made all too often. Love is something you give away to others. Love is not exclusive. It does not make one special or another more special. Love does not divide or conquer or exclude anyone. It embraces change and grows with differences. It is these times when we unite, but maintain our uniqueness. Grow and guide through synergy and see all of the commonalities people really do share. In this sharing we become wiser in our knowledge and love for others. We give each other pieces of our wisdom through giving. Excitement comes in giving at all times for there is love. One must love thyself before you can offer anything to anyone. We need to know love from within and then share it with others. All we need to do is look within for the divine and feel God's guidance. Know God helps you to breathe. You don't even need to try. Just be conscious of your breathing and see how much love you give to yourself. Then share it generously with everybody in prayer and with all whom you come into contact -- through your business contacts, through your friends and family, whoever that may be. Especially remember those in your heart you do not know. Give your love away to everyone.

* * *

Visualize and 'pray peace' in this world. Leave no one behind. Practice breathing properly. Learn to connect with your internal God and work toward creating peace in your world and the world around us.

* * *

Always ask yourself questions that will empower you. What did I learn today? How have I grown? Where have I invested my thoughts? Was I kind to myself and others? How can I improve my smile? How have I improved my loving kindness and compassion and care for others? Am I living my life based on peace that will bring me joy? Ask yourself these empowering questions and even in the evening ask yourself whose lives have I impacted today and how did it change us both. Send love to those people you have a tough time with and pray to them. Write a letter stamped with love and compassion and a willingness to reconcile your strained relationship. You may not wish to send that letter, but it's the intention of writing the letter. Ask yourself what have I learned today that I did not know yesterday. Sit silent for awhile and sit to the peaceful and practical answers that will come to you.

* * *

Happiness comes in caring about others. Once we care about others, we will also have happiness generated within ourselves. It never works the other way. Bring peace to the family by bringing and finding peace within yourself. Listen to what others feel and truly listen and care. And in doing so, you show your love and care. This makes them happy and inevitably, of course, this will also make you feel good about yourself, too.

❀ ❀ ❀

Remember the analogy of the tunnel. Remember to go slowly in the tunnel. The analogy I like to use is a train going through the tunnel. As you slow the train down, be in your emotions. Feel the negative emotions that you're feeling or the darkness and allow the train to slow down. And as it slows down, allow room to grow and be in your feelings before you let it go gently to a new profound thought pattern. Then you will see the light at the end of the tunnel.

❀ ❀ ❀

A poem: Seed only the good. May God fly by your feet, trickle through your toes, and you will find love where everybody goes. Have a great day.

❀ ❀ ❀

Have a great day and know you can do everything & anything. Know that you will find love where everyone goes. And in knowing you can do anything & everything, you will achieve all the things that are possible in this world, which starts with you every day.

❀ ❀ ❀

Know in spirit we grow and in flesh we flow. Combine them together and we maintain balance and spirit on earth, the balance between spirit and the material world. We are one with God and know that in doing so we can achieve anything & everything in our world. Keep remembering God.

❀ ❀ ❀

Keep remembering God in everything you do and everything that you are and in everything you can be.

❀ ❀ ❀

Remember that guilt is a wasted energy that gets us nowhere and remember that pride is not love. Love is a much more powerful energy than pride. Follow your heart and know you can do anything & everything that is your truest desire to be the best that you can be and follow that to the T.

* * *

Believe in thyself, believe in God, believe in nature, believe in ourselves. We sometimes need objects such as beads to help us believe in ourselves. We need beads because we're having a hard time believing in ourselves. The beads won't change us, but they will surely soothe us, allowing us to be quiet, be silent, and to love ourselves. Loving ourselves and believing in ourselves, involving communication of any form is important. So as we share and become more loving to ourselves, we give to others. In giving we learn to forgive. When we feel we cannot forgive, we need to remember that anyone with discipline knows we can do anything and change anything & everything in our lives. It is up to us for all things are possible with God.

* * *

Remember, something good will come out of everything. As we remember, something good is going to come out of this. We're allowed to feel the negative emotion or thought or circumstance and say something good is going to come out of this. And this allows us to remember there is something to be learned in every situation.

* * *

As we remember that something good is going to come out of everything, we realize that everything is infinitely guided and all in divine order.

* * *

As we understand that we are the creator of our world, then we understand that we have only one choice, but to be happy with what we created.

* * *

As we learn that we can create everything in our own world, we also understand our world is what matters. Whether we sit down and look at a blade of grass or whether we enjoy the breeze of the ocean or whether we sit in our office building and look at the sun as it rises above our office window. Whatever it may be, always know that you choose to create whatever you wish in your own world. So today, be the creator of your own world. Have a great day.

❀ ❀ ❀

When you know who you are, you know that the essence of who you are is from within your heart. And as a child you always knew who you were. And just remember you look at a picture of when you were young, that's who you are. Keep creating more of that abundance through the infinite possibilities that you remember as a child. Do the same and have the same dreams and the same visions as an adult.

❀ ❀ ❀

Children may feel that they are unable to do things without their parents. But in reality, parents are usually unable to do things without their children. And it is important to remember that we must not live vicariously by our children's success, but we need to be there to guide them and to be there as true friends and support. In doing so, we understand the unconditional love that is needed for a child and that the child who is growing as an adult already has the true essence of who they are within them. Always let them know that they are great ones and their divine purpose is within them and they need only seek it for themselves and only ask within what their true divine purpose truly is.

❀ ❀ ❀

Give everyone the opportunity to be the infinite divine self. Allow people to be more of who they are when they're around you. Then truly you're being their best friend and you're being a true best friend to yourself.

❀ ❀ ❀

When we give our friends love, we give ourselves the permission to live in peace.

❀ ❀ ❀

Inner peace is the key.

❀ ❀ ❀

Within each one of us is the ability to be free and to live from that place of love.

❀ ❀ ❀

Without inner peace, there is no harmony. And without harmony, there is no joy.

❀ ❀ ❀

Acknowledgments

To God ~ that inner Divine that allows us to Do ANYTHING & EVERYTHING including this very book which we hold now.

Thank you God... you have given us all the Power to look within and make a difference in other people's lives by sharing in the Light of God that is within us all. All this is Possible with our own ability to Awaken the inner Power residing Within US All.

The light Shines in us all: Let the Hero Come out and play in all of us ~ reaching out Beyond the moon and amongst the stars in a kindly and loving way we reach to others and in being with others we are allowing each other the ability and opportunity to achieve all of our endeavours. We help each other to look within and see beyond our bodies and create 'inter-independent relationships' with all those around us. As we tap into our own resources we see how we are so important and we are all so Great and true Geniuses.

Furthermore, "With community we create unity" and make beautiful loving Bonds with one another based on the purest intent to help one another Grow; with all our neighbors and colleagues in business and abroad we salvage these relationships and hold them dear to our hearts knowing we have attracted this to us to serve one another's purpose. But Remembering with the individual comes the community to support the individual vision. But without the community there is no individual and without individuals there is no community.

It is for this reason we acknowledge all those who have supported and helped in bringing this book together. "TRUE FRIENDS help you BECOME more of who you are in (their Presence) and in your own Presence".

And thus to all who also Contributed to this book's success and all the DVD's and Audio CD's and seminars that come with all of this, THANK YOU in Loving Gratitude.

You Know who you are. Much Love, Honor and Respect is Given to you and accepted by your Great love and help along the way. This Peace of ours is in all of us. And By sharing and knowing what to do we were able to put together something that will change how the world changes with us as we change our thoughts and lead by example with our hearts: Children understand monkey see monkey do; whether we do it or not, we still feel it and follow our mentors' or parents' footsteps. So we all need individuals that will allow us to see things another way. BUT first we need to be willing, ready and able to make those changes ourselves. Thank you to all, for making this possible, with such Dear friends at hand, you Give love and light with understanding, good conversation, relinquishing judgment while still being a true Friend. The world needs more friends like you. For this We are all so eternally appreciative with much love given and received. God really successfully works through us when we align with what is to be the law of attraction.

You all have been thanked individually for your efforts and heart of Gold filled with love to Give and Serve others thus making our communities happy and fulfilled. When we help please others we will find others will help us too. WE ARE all dependent on this "inter-independence" (which is in the new books to be discussed further), which will help us all to see the oneness of it all and appreciate how we all have VERY simple and common Principles…. We all are people of Principle at heart, which allows us to be at peace with life, even through the challenges since we Grasp onto each other and help each other advance, flow, grow and enhance each other's inner God Given Powers.

Children have this and we, as adults must allow Children to continually see this GREATNESS as the GENIUSES of our

Generations to come. Thank you to you all for making the Genius in us Grow in this Very book and in sharing in other ways.

You are all Appreciated & Loved for your Countless input, time, expertise, love & willingness to MAKE change possible in each other's lives – TRUE friends allow us to Be More of who we are in each other's presence. You all have served with Purpose & given from that sincere place: You have given from A Sincere & very pure intention of the Heart. For this we are all Eternally Grateful – in infinite And Avalanches of Abundance, like the never-ending waves of the ocean and sand that we all can play on.

Much Love to You All,
Aloha & Mahalo!
Love Always,
Peter Sammarco
November 22, 2006

P.S. the words are written in a way that is to emphasize certain points (i.e. Capitalized words and dashes) and are not a grammatical error at all...so have fun and enjoy in joy. This is complete, we are all perfect just the way we are.

About the Author:

Peter Sammarco knows this: we are one, and capable of doing everything and anything. It is from this knowing, and from his own personal odyssey, that he shares the secrets that need to be awakened within us all. Whether in his writing, or through his service with CanPeace Consultants Inc., Peter delivers practical help for growing true success in daily life.

Contact CanPeace Consultants today for personal, business, trade or political-related products, services, or relationship building at...

www.HealYourself.ca.

email: peter@fivepillars.ca

If you would like information about Peter Sammarco's
workshops and seminars, keynote speaking, or to order
copies of his books, CD's, DVD's or tapes, please contact:

CanPeace Consultants Catalogues
Post Office Box 73555
1014 Robson St.
Vancouver, BC V6E 4L9
Canada

Or The Bentall Building by calling: 604-676-3555

www.HealYourself.ca

peter@fivepillars.ca

ISBN 142512437-2